Let's Travel in
JAPAN

Edited by Darlene Geis

A TRAVEL PRESS BOOK

PICTURE ACKNOWLEDGMENTS
The full-color illustrations in this book were taken in Japan by Ace Williams. For the black-and-white photographs, we wish to thank the Japan Tourist Association; Werner Bischof, Marc Riboud and Denis Stock from Magnum; the Naval Historical Foundation, Library of Congress; and Ace Williams. The map was made by Enrico Arno.

THIRD PRINTING

Original copyright, © 1960 by Columbia Record Club, Inc., New York, N. Y.
under the title of *A Colorslide Tour of Japan*. All rights reserved.
New edition published 1965 by CHILDRENS PRESS, INC., Chicago.
Published simultaneously in Canada.   Lithographed in the U.S.A.
Library of Congress Catalog Card Number: 65-12226

CONTENTS

CHINA
U.S.S.R.
KOREA
JAPAN SEA
JAPAN ALPS
HON
MT. FUJI
Miyajima
28
29
Hiroshima
27
17
14-16
Kyoto
Nara
Shodo I.
22
23
18-21
Osaka
12
13
Kamakura
8
Hakone
9
10
Inland Sea
1
Takamatsu
26
24
25
Kochi
30-32
Nagasaki
KYUSHU
SHIKOKU
PACIF

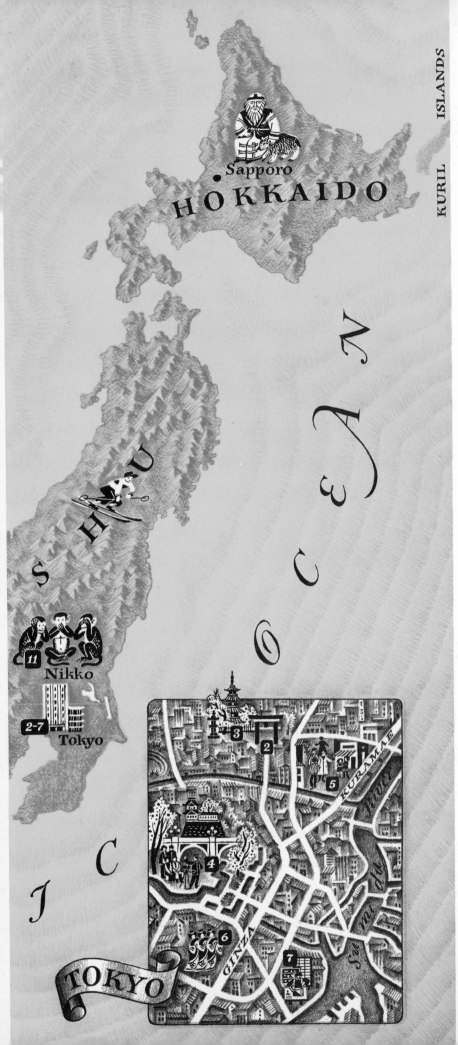

Locales of thirty-two full-page pictures

JAPAN, LAND OF THE RISING SUN

J UST beyond the coast of northeast Asia the islands of Japan stand guard like an Oriental dragon looking eastward across the Pacific. Issuing from the dragon's mouth is a long plume of smoke —a string of tiny islets called the Kurils (koo-*reels*), which were taken over by Russia after World War II. It is somehow very fitting that this exotic land should take the shape of a legendary dragon of the East. For Japan, isolated for so many centuries from the rest of the world, retained in a completely unadulterated form the quaintness and strangeness of the Orient. In the last century, though she has taken on Western ways at an amazing rate, the old traditions are still preserved, coloring much of the life of modern Japan. It is this combination of the old and the new that is so fascinating. The ancient dragon has become streamlined before our very eyes.

Although Japan is made up of over three thousand islands, there are four main islands that concern us. Northernmost Hokkaido (*hoh*-kye-*doh*) is the head of the dragon. Honshu (hohn-*shoo*), or the mainland, is its body. Shikoku (*shih*-koh-*koo*) forms its hind legs, while Kyushu (kyoo-*shoo*) dipping down to the south is the dragon's tail. Japan is a little smaller than the state of California, yet it must support a population of over 91,000,000 people. This is perhaps one reason why the dragon has hungrily tried to gobble nearby territory time and again in the last half century.

Japan, besides being small, is a country of many mountains. The tallest of them is Fuji, cone-shaped symbol of this lovely land. Verdant and fertile, the landscape is one of thrusting peaks and narrow valleys. Its very beauty is a disguise for the hardship imposed by the majestic mountains. Because of them, only about 15 per cent of the land is flat enough to cultivate. So the Japanese have had to develop a patient genius for coaxing the maximum yield from every inch of arable land. Their skill at nurturing growing things is legendary, and it was acquired because of the difficult nature of their country.

THE PEOPLE OF JAPAN

The Ainus are primitive survivors of a prehistoric people who were the first inhabitants of Japan.

The inhabitants of these green and mountainous islands have physical characteristics we all know well. They are short of stature, with the high cheekbones, straight black hair, and light yellowish-brown skin typical of Mongoloid peoples. Yet the original settlers of the Japanese archipelago were probably a white-skinned people who traveled down from Siberia across the steppingstones of the Kuril Islands about 5,000 years ago. These primitive hunters have left their traces all the way down to Kyushu. But they were driven from the southern islands by later invasions of the more advanced Mongoloid people from Korea, China and the South Seas. The aborigines were scornfully described as people who "gathered like ants to attack, but scattered like birds as soon as you faced them." Today the descendants of those earliest Japanese, the Ainus (EYE-*nooz*), are to be found only in Hokkaido, the snowy northernmost island. They are bearded, white-skinned and strong-featured, a type very different from the Japanese we know.

The present-day Japanese have a great charm for the visitor to their gracious land. Theirs is a delicacy, not only of physical form but of manner as well, that is utterly captivating. Japanese women, in particular, with their doll-like daintiness and their self-effacing desire to please, are enchanting—ask any Western man who has met one. The waitresses and chambermaids and store clerks with whom a traveler comes in contact are smiling ambassadors for their country. Nowhere in the world is courtesy practiced with such exquisite artistry as in Japan.

THE JAPANESE FAMILY

To a Westerner the elaborate bows and smiles and flowery phrases of greeting may seem exaggerated, but they have been bred into the Japanese through centuries of regulations and laws. It all starts with the family, whose undisputed head is papa. Wives obey husbands, younger people obey older people, and there are special forms of

10

courtesy to be used when addressing each social level. At table, for example, papa is served first. Next in line is the eldest son, who takes precedence over all the children. If there are infants in the family, they are served after the eldest son but ahead of the second son, and for that reason the Number Two Boy is sometimes jestingly referred to as "Master Cold Rice." Under this system everyone knows his place and there are no arguments.

Filial piety is one of the great virtues of Japanese life, extending into the ancestor worship of their religion and obedience to the emperor. Old people are treated with respect and affection, and a favorite story tells of this crowning example of loyalty to one's parents: In ancient China there was once a man in his sixties who used to put on the clothes of a child and play on the floor with his toys, to beguile his failing parents into feeling young again. The entire concept of the family society came to Japan from China in the teachings of Confucius, and it influences Japanese customs and thought today.

LESSONS FROM CHINA

Even to the casual observer Japan's cultural debt to China is obvious. To begin with, China named the islands to the east of her the "land of the Rising Sun," and to this day the Japanese call their own country Nippon, a version of the Chinese name. Japan's written language is based on Chinese ideograms, yet it is not the same as Chinese. The Japanese kimono has evolved from the loose-sleeved Chinese robe, but it has become an entirely different garment. For her architecture, her art and even her unique gardens, Japan owes a great deal to China, who first introduced the primitive Japanese to a far older civilization.

But it was in the sixth century that the single most influential cultural exchange took place. It was then that Buddhism was brought into Japan from the mainland. At that time the Japanese religion was Shinto, or "the way of the Gods." It was an ancient faith whose mythology taught the isolated islanders that they were indeed a people apart, whose emperor was a divinity directly descended from the sun-goddess.

Buddhism, with its more elaborate temples, its statuary and paintings, and its philosophical writings, immeasurably enriched the Japanese culture, which up until the sixth century had been fairly barren. And this Chinese heritage has also added to the Japanese landscape the gorgeous temples and graceful pagodas we see silhouetted against mountain and forest. Buddhism and Shinto now exist side by side, and most Japanese embrace both.

THE WESTERN AWAKENING

After absorbing so much of China's great old civilization, in the ninth century the Japanese shut themselves away within their small islands. The emperor, while still divine, became just a figurehead, and the country was really run by military governors called shoguns (SHOW-*goons*). Until the middle of the nineteenth century, Japan dreamed on unchanged, a feudal empire that remained aloof from the outside world, her islands closed to all but a handful of foreigners.

The exceptions were occasional British, Dutch and Portuguese traders. And a handful of intrepid missionaries introduced certain Western customs to the Japanese in their own gentle way. But the most dramatic gesture of all—generally taken to symbolize the "opening" of Japan—was made one July day in 1853 when Commodore Matthew Perry and his "black ships" steamed toward Tokyo Bay. A year later Perry officially opened Japan to commerce with the United States, and the fresh winds of Western civilization blew through a country that was liberated at last from her long self-imprisonment.

Perry's "black ships," belching smoke and roiling up the waters, struck terror into the hearts of the Japanese.

In the half century following Perry's bold expedition, Japan rocketed upward in a brilliant burst of progress under the Emperor Meiji (MAY-*jee*). The laggard country awoke and built a network of railways, a banking system and a merchant marine. With the same avidity which she had shown centuries before for Chinese culture, Japan absorbed Western technology, and developed industries and institutions patterned after ours.

Japan was an industrial world power to be reckoned with by the time the twentieth century dawned. But then the militarists became strong again, and at their instigation Japan embarked on a program of wars that culminated in her defeat in 1945.

THE TWO WORLDS OF JAPAN

In spite of the rush of Western ways and ideas that have swept through Japan creating great changes, there is still a picturesque foundation of the ancient and traditional that exists side by side with the modern. We see it when we arrive at Tokyo, the nation's capital and now the largest city in the world. It has skyscrapers and department stores, factories, smokestacks, elevated trains, traffic snarls, neon lights, bars, honky-tonks, slums, theaters and parks—all the mixed blessings of a Western twentieth-century city. Like a green and peaceful island at the heart of this hurly-burly are the moated grounds of the Imperial Palace. Old Japan has a way of peeping out from behind the new.

It is possible today to travel from the big cities to the fairyland of the Japanese countryside, and be transported backward in time to old Japan. Here is the landscape recognized from a hundred Japanese prints—the steep mountains, the mysterious forests, the serene fields, cultivated in neat small plots, surrounding a graceful peasant house that nestles under its peaked roof of thatch.

We can make a pilgrimage to the earliest permanent capital of Japan, the classical city of Nara (NAH-*rah*). Below its wooded slopes the city today is a living museum of eighth-century Japan. We see it not as a collection of well-preserved ruins but alive and beautiful, almost as it was in the years of its glory. As we look up at the sweeping roofs of the pagodas we, too, can feel the vitality and inspiration that came to Japan 1,200 years ago from China and first took root and flowered here at Nara.

It is these glimpses of exotic Japan that the visitor cherishes. But the modern young people in Tokyo and the big cities prefer Western ways. Their clothes, their taste in music (rock-and-roll is a big fad), art and movies, their fast motorcycles—all are borrowed from Europe and the United States. Japan today still seems to take greater pride in her new industrial empire than in the glories of her old emperors.

THE CULT OF THE BEAUTIFUL

Visitors to this island empire might at first be concerned with its overwhelming strangeness. If they begin their travels in Tokyo, the ugly and sordid aspects of a fast-growing big city might give them a false impression of Japan. But before very long the visitor becomes aware of the underlying grace and beauty inherent in much of Japanese life.

The Japanese house, built of wood and paper, has a light strength and a simple uncluttered beauty that is beginning to exert an enormous influence on our own domestic architecture. The chaste Japanese garden that creates a whole small world in a tiny plot of ground is pleasing to Western eyes surfeited with a riot of rosebushes and filigreed flower beds.

The tourist in Japan soon finds himself enchanted at every turn. A rainy day causes the grey streets to light up with delicate and brightly colored paper umbrellas. A Japanese room, bare except for straw matting and a low, lacquered table, comes to life because of the perfect placement of three blossoms in a vase. An evening at the theater, though the language is incomprehensible, is a feast for the eyes because of the fabulous costuming and elegant attitudes of the players. The shrines to alien gods and strange faiths stir the feelings if only because of their intrinsic harmony and beauty.

As we travel through Japan we will fall more and more under its spell. And with an aesthetic appreciation of Japanese beauty comes the first bridge to an understanding of the country and its people.

Wood and paper and straw combine to make a house of elegant simplicity—peaceful and soul-satisfying.

let's travel in

JAPAN

JAPANESE LANDSCAPE: AN ORIENTAL FAIRYLAND

THIS is the classic picture of old Japan. It is the scene we are most likely to imagine when we think of this quaint and charming country as it used to be. But as we stand here in a wooded dell, we are amazed that old Japan really exists today, the actuality matching our fantasy in every detail. Outside the big industrial centers that have put Japan in the forefront of modern nations, the country still looks like this.

Here are the verdant mountains shrouded in mist, the squat trees spreading their umbrella-shaped branches close to the ground. We could not have imagined a more perfect bridge than this one, its simple wooden arch reflected in the green water of the pond. And surely if we had peopled our imaginary landscape, we would have had a few delicate, kimono-clad girls mincing across the little bridge, too. But these are real girls, and they have paused under their gay parasols to feed the carp and goldfish that live in the quiet pond.

The serene countryside with its dreamlike atmosphere is endlessly diverting. The land is broken up into thousands of hidden valleys, and views like this one are typical. This scene is on the island of Shikoku near the Inland Sea, but it might be anywhere in Japan. There are no broad vistas or distant horizons here. Instead, everything is reduced to miniature proportions, and grace and simplicity delight the eye without overwhelming it.

The natural beauty of their country inspired and nurtured a feeling for the beautiful in the Japanese people, and love of nature has become a national characteristic. No other people makes a festival of moon-viewing, insect-listening and cherry-blossom-gazing. And in the cities devoted to industrial progress, the private gardens and public parks re-create this timeless countryside for those who are shut away from it in a modern metropolis.

16

UENO PARK: GARDEN SPOT IN TOKYO

WE ARE in the Japanese capital now, and although it is the largest city in the world, with its fair share of steel and concrete buildings, Tokyo still is an intermingling of ancient and modern. We can see both in this picture where a girl in Western sweater-and-skirt and bobby socks is striding along the path, while in the opposite direction a Japanese woman dressed in the traditional kimono walks with tiny pigeon-toed steps. Both have probably come to Ueno (oo-*eh-noh*) Park to see the cherry trees in bloom, a sight that has special significance for all Japanese.

For the two weeks in April when the pink blossoms brighten the land, a holiday spirit pervades Japan. The parks are jammed with people who admire the fragile flowers. The beauty of the cherry blossom is enhanced for the Japanese because it is of such short duration, and their feeling for their national flower is expressed by this poem which every child learns in school:

> "Though the color be fragrant
> The flower will fall:
> Who in this world of ours
> Will last forever?"

In spite of this rather glum thought, the cherry-blossom season is a time of merrymaking and festivity, and the park will be filled with picnickers feasting under the trees heedless of thoughts of flowerless tomorrows.

Although Ueno Park is open to the public now, it was formerly a vast private estate where the family shrine of the Tokugawa (*too-koo-*GAH-*wah*) shoguns was situated. The gateway in the background is called a torii (TOE-*ree*), and this simple crossbar arrangement is seen all over Japan at the entrance to every Shinto shrine.

FIVE-STORY PAGODA: SHRINE IN UENO PARK

FOLLOWING the avenue of cherry trees we come to the Toshogu (*toh-*SHOH-*goo*) Shrine, and in this picture we see the five-story pagoda silhouetted against an April sky. The shrine was built in memory of one of Japan's great feudal leaders, the shogun Iyeyasu (*ee-yeh-*YAH-*soo*) Tokugawa. In the seventeenth century Iyeyasu established his capital at Tokyo— it was then called Edo (*eh-*DOH)—and he founded a line of military governors who ruled Japan until the Mikado's powers were restored in the last half of the nineteenth century.

In the foreground two massive stone lanterns stand like sentinels before the pagoda. There are usually armies of these stone or bronze lanterns lined up near all Buddhist and Shinto shrines. Originally they were put there to light the grounds, but eventually their purpose became purely decorative. During the military dictatorship of the Tokugawas, courtiers and lords of outlying provinces tried to outdo one another in gifts of stone lanterns.

There are three hundred of these oddly shaped monuments on the grounds of this shrine at Ueno Park. All of them are arranged with military precision in neat ranks. But there is one lantern twice as large as the others, and it stands off by itself. The reason it is separated from the rest of the lanterns reflects the class distinctions made in feudal Japan—it was the gift not of a noble lord but of an ordinary samurai (SAM-*uh-rye*), or warrior.

There is a charming little superstition about this king-size lantern. It is believed that if a child hops on one leg all the way around the base, the wooden clog that is left behind will be snatched away by an unseen spirit. As a result the samurai's gift is known as a "spook lantern." The supernatural plays a large part in Japanese folklore, and the susceptible visitor can almost believe that there really are spirits lurking near the shadowy shrines.

21

IMPERIAL PALACE: PICTURESQUE LANDMARK

I N THE heart of modern Tokyo, surrounded by a chain of moats, stands the quiet green island of the Imperial Palace. Developed in the seventeenth century, this 250-acre tract of ground held the castle and court of the Tokugawa shoguns. The Emperor, divine but powerless, had his court in the ancient capital of Kyoto (кчон-*toh*). It was not until after Commodore Perry opened Japan that the Emperor Meiji assumed his rightful role as ruler and moved into this Imperial Palace.

Here the Emperor and his family live, secluded from the raucous traffic and bustle of the city. In 1946 the Emperor issued a revolutionary proclamation denying his divinity. Since then, it has become imperial custom for the Emperor to mingle with his people as any mortal ruler may. And on special days such as the New Year the general public is even permitted to enter the sacrosanct grounds of the Palace to greet him.

On other days the moated island is still the number-one tourist

On the streets of modern Tokyo the honorable bow is made—survival of an ancient courtesy.

attraction of Tokyo. All the sightseeing buses stop near the Double Bridge, and everyone clambers out for a view of the bold masonry walls and the proud white swans floating below them. Then the group lines up to have a souvenir picture taken. Our picture has caught a busload of tourists just as they are watching the birdie—or the Japanese equivalent thereof. The serious schoolboys in their somber black uniforms are a common sight in Japan, and the photographer will not try to make them smile.

22

ASAKUSA SECTION: STREET OF AMUSEMENTS

SOMETIMES it seems that most of Tokyo's nine million inhabitants are thronging to the narrow streets of Asakusa (*ah-*SAHK*-sah*) in search of entertainment. This tiny city-within-a-city originally grew up around a temple dedicated to Kannon (*kahn-nohn*), Goddess of Mercy. The old temple still stands amidst the swirl of merrymaking humanity, but the theaters and shops of the neighborhood cut it off from view.

This is one of the most colorful sections of Tokyo, festooned with banners and neon signs and bright paper lanterns. A whole row of movie houses competes with the live entertainment—you can see the Japanese Roxy on the right in this picture—and American and European motion pictures are extremely popular.

In spring, cherry trees are not the only things to burst into bright blossom in Japan. The amusement centers and especially the theaters flower with brilliant musical revues. After the bleak and chilly Japanese winter, the country is once again clothed in bright colors, and the mild weather invites people out of doors. They find their entertainment in gay streets like this one, and those who can, flock to the popular musical theaters to see the spring revues. We are going to look in on the most famous of these entertainments—the Takarazuka (*tah-kah-*RAHZ*-kah*) Opera Troupe on tour in Tokyo.

25

GIRLS, GIRLS, GIRLS: THE TAKARAZUKA TROUPE

WE ARE watching the prologue of "Spring Dance: Tales of Japanese Love," and in this scene the enormous stage is filled with 58 girls dressed in the costume of young apprentice geishas (GAY-*shahs*). In Tokyo the Takarazuka Troupe performs at two-month intervals at the Tokyo Taka Theater, a huge auditorium formerly celebrated as the Ernie Pyle Theater.

The story of the Takarazuka girls was immortalized by novelist James Michener in *Sayonara*. This is the troupe that comes from the little resort town of Takarazuka about 45 minutes from Osaka (OH-*sah-kah*). Early in this century the railway line connecting the two towns needed some sort of attraction to increase traffic to and from Takarazuka. The Opera Troupe and its theater were the answer. Today they have their own Opera House which seats 4,000 people, and there is a special music school where girls are given a difficult two-year training course. Their discipline and dedication are legendary.

The troupe is able to perform the traditional dramas of Japan and its folk dances, but they make an even greater splash with their

The Takarazuka girls spend long hours in school acquiring the grace that seems to come naturally.

versions of Western musicals. The fact that both male and female parts are acted by beautiful Oriental girls adds to the piquancy of the performance, and watching their show we can understand why the Takarazuka girls are idolized by Japan's teen-age set.

26

MAKING A
WOOD-BLOCK PRINT:
JAPAN'S
GREAT ART

THE honky-tonk amusements and cheap souvenirs of present-day Japan are only surface flotsam on the deep clear waters of her traditional culture. In the shops of Tokyo you can buy the fine objects for which Japanese craftsmen and artists have long been famous—porcelain, brocaded silks, carved ivory, cloisonné, lacquer ware, and the prints that have pictured the beauties of Japanese life for hundreds of years.

This picture shows the studio of one of the modern print makers, who is using a technique that has been handed down for generations. The artist's picture is pasted upon a block of cherry wood, and a skilled engraver then chisels out the design. A different block is made for each color used, and in a complex picture as many as twenty blocks are carved for the different colors needed. On the shelves behind this man we can see dozens of little bowls, each containing a brightly hued ink. The brush near the artist's hand is used to apply the color to the wood block, and the printing is done by pressing a sheet of paper against the block. The feeling and skill with which the printer makes this impression contribute much to the finished picture. As he tenderly peels this sheet from the block, our printmaker seems pleased with the result, although obviously there are many more details and colors still to come.

The woodcut technique was originally brought to Japan from China where it had been used for printing Buddhist texts and illustrations. The earliest printed texts still surviving in the world are some Japanese Buddhist charms printed in the eighth century, seven hundred years before Gutenberg's Bible. Later the Japanese developed wood-block printing into an extraordinarily popular art form. Called "Passing World Pictures," the great prints of the eighteenth and nineteenth centuries depicted actors, beautiful girls and landscapes, and were inexpensively produced for the lower classes. Today those old prints are highly prized, and can be seen in many of the world's great art museums.

GREAT BUDDHA OF INFINITE LIGHT: KAMAKURA WONDER

JAPANESE artists have also excelled at sculpture, and in this picture we are standing before the most famous statue in all Japan, the Great Buddha of Kamakura (*kah*-MAH-*koo-rah*). In 1252 when the calm bronze giant was erected, Kamakura was the military capital of the country. Today this beach resort just thirty miles from Tokyo is a Japanese Coney Island, swarming with weekend bathers, but still presided over by the dignified and contemplative Buddha.

The statue's hands rest on its lap with palms turned up and thumbs touching, the symbolic posture of steadfast faith. Towering 42½ feet above the ground, the Great Buddha inclines his head slightly and gazes down from half-closed eyes at the people below him. Worshipers say that his gaze penetrates to their very soul, and the two women in blue seem to be held by his brooding stare.

Originally the Buddha was housed in a wooden building, but typhoons and tidal waves wrecked the structure, leaving the great

The frosty cone of Mt. Fuji rises in simple grandeur above the Japanese countryside.

image serenely unharmed. For nearly five hundred years the Great Buddha of Infinite Light has sat under the open sky, untouched by natural disasters, wars or changing times. Perry's ships anchored near Kamakura, but the old capital was off limits to the Americans and they never saw this ancient marvel. After the Second World War, Allied soldiers in Japan flocked to visit the Buddha—an image of perfect peace to refresh the war-weary.

PALANQUIN CARRIERS: HAKONE DISTRICT

NOT far from where Mt. Fuji's snow-topped cone rises above the landscape is the lovely resort district of Hakone (*hah-koh*-NEH). The hot springs, the mountain lake and the attractive inns of the neighborhood make it a popular vacation spot. But three hundred years ago this area was important because it lay on the main road between Kyoto and Tokyo. In those days a barrier was set up at Hakone where travelers going from one section of the country to another had to present identification and credentials. The Tokugawa shoguns added to the normal traffic. They kept their lords under control by requiring them to leave their families as hostages in Tokyo while the lords themselves spent alternate years commuting between the capital and their home preserves. So the mountain road near Hakone was often the scene of colorful processions to and from Tokyo as the feudal lords and their retinues passed to and fro on their "in" and "out" years.

When the men in this picture were young, they earned their livelihood carrying people over the mountain passes where other vehicles could not penetrate. Now in their eighties, these men are a living link with feudal times. Roads have been improved and this primitive form of transportation is no longer used, but occasionally the old boys like to get into their climbing outfits and bring out their ancient kago (*kah*-GOH). Kago literally means basket, but specifically it is the name given to the bamboo or wicker seat slung from a pole carried by two men. And that third man bringing up the rear and apparently doing nothing is actually there to pull on a straw rope attached to the front part of the pole on the upgrade, and to hold back on the rear rope on the downgrade. Sometimes he just goes along for the ride, especially when the rider is a pretty girl young enough to be his great-granddaughter. But for all their years these fellows are sturdy and muscular, and the machine-age specimens who come to Hakone for the hot baths will never be their match.

INN NEAR
HAKONE:
UNCEREMONIAL TEA

OUT on the balcony of a Japanese-style inn, with the pine-clad mountains as a backdrop, an outdoor tea party is taking place. One of the charms of traveling in this country is the opportunity—especially in the resort areas—of staying at a Japanese inn. In these inns you remove your shoes at the door, sit on the floor which is covered with soft straw matting called tatami (*tah-tah-*MEE), sleep on a low pile of quilts, eat at a foot-high table, and acquire a refreshing change of perspective.

You can also be introduced to the institution of the Japanese bath, providing your Western reticence permits it. The Japanese have none of our scruples about nudity, and their baths are large tanks filled with steaming hot water and people of both sexes and all ages. Washing is done *before* you get into the bath, and it is followed by a long luxurious soak in the clean though populous water. Not everybody's cup of tea.

Nor is tea itself, when served in the ancient ceremonial manner. These young people are having an informal tea, but one of the cherished arts of a cultivated Japanese is the ability to perform the formal ritual of the tea ceremony. Centuries ago certain Zen Buddhist priests raised the drinking of a cup of tea to the status of a ceremony. The arrangement of simple utensils and the delicacy and precision with which every gesture is performed has become a high art now, taught by revered tea-masters. The tea itself has the consistency of a thick pea soup. The ritual takes several hours, and few Westerners can appreciate it. But its Japanese practitioners feel that the tea ceremony is conducive to poise, tranquillity, courtesy and harmony, the Buddhist virtues to which they aspire. For the visitor to Japan it is at the very least a fascinating insight into another culture.

THREE WISE MONKEYS: CARVING AT NIKKO

NINETY miles north of Tokyo is the fabulous Nikko (*nih-koh*) National Park. Here in a setting of scenic grandeur ancient trees, waterfalls, mountains and lakes combine with a group of the most magnificent shrines in Japan. When the great shogun Iyeyasu Tokugawa died, he was buried at Nikko, and the finest artists and craftsmen were gathered from all over Japan to compete in the building of shrines in his memory. Most of the wooden structures are intricately carved and gilded, and enough gold leaf to cover six acres was used. The Japanese, awed by the double glories wrought by nature and man, sum it up with this saying, "Never say *kekko* (magnificent) until you've seen Nikko."

We are looking at the famous simian threesome on one of the more modest of the shrine buildings, the Sacred Stable. It is the only structure that is not lacquered, but its beautifully weathered wood sets off the carved and painted decorations better than the shiny vermilion of the neighboring buildings. This group is known as "the monkeys of the three countries," and in the seventeenth century the trio was originally supposed to represent India, China and Japan. "Hear no evil, speak no evil, see no evil." Horse sense from the walls of the Sacred Stable!

A line of Shinto priests in ancient costume ascends the stairway to their holy shrine.

37

KASUGA SHRINE:
IN THE FOREST
OF NARA

WE HAVE traveled westward from Tokyo to Japan's first capital, the classical city of Nara. Before the eighth century Japan had no permanent capital. Every time an emperor died the court had to move to a different city. But in 710 the Empress Gemmyo (GHEM-*yoh*) succeeded her own son to the Japanese throne after his brief reign. Possibly her housewifely instincts revolted at the prospect of moving again, and so she put her regal little foot down and Nara remained the capital for many splendid decades. During this period the arts flourished, and the city grew great and beautiful, modeled as it was after the finest Chinese cities of the time.

Today Nara is much smaller and quieter than it was in its heyday, but we can still see in its ambitious buildings and varied treasures the surge of progress that carried Japan to new heights. In this picture we become aware again of the Japanese genius for blending nature and art. The Kasuga (*kah*-soo-*gah*) Shrine is a venerable Shinto shrine

Religious festivals are gay and noisy, as elaborate shrine cars are pulled through crowded streets.

founded twelve hundred years ago. Its swooping roofs and clear vermilion color are particularly well suited to its setting in an ancient forest. The shrine consists of four small buildings, bravely painted, and approached through rows of stone lanterns—some three thousand of them. Twice a year on special festivals these lanterns are lit, and they glow like fireflies among the dark old trees and graceful buildings.

38

ANCIENT BUDDHA: TREASURED IMAGE

IN THE National Museum of Nara there is a collection of many of the finest works of art dating from the great Nara Period (645-781). Among the treasures is this noble Buddha head looking as fresh and vibrant as the artfully arranged flowers on its pedestal. During the Nara Period Buddha was the favorite sculptural subject. Images were made by the thousands, carved from wood and modeled in clay as well as cast in bronze.

One of the most remarkable achievements of the age—or of any other age, for that matter—was the casting of the largest bronze statue in the world, the Daibutsu (*dye-boo*-TSOO), or Great Buddha of Nara. In 735 a terrible smallpox epidemic ravaged Japan, and many of the people in the capital fell prey to it. The Emperor was a devout man, and he decided that a colossal image of Buddha would be necessary to dispel such a widespread epidemic. The construction of the Daibutsu became a national project, since they needed over four hundred tons of bronze and huge quantities of other materials to cast this epic statue. After eight attempts over a four-year period the great seated figure was finally completed successfully.

Then the Emperor was faced with the problem of gilding his Buddha —no small undertaking, since the statue was over fifty-three feet high. There wasn't enough gold in his entire country for the job. But at the propitious moment the precious metal was discovered in the distant forests where the Ainus lived. The Great Buddha was then encased in 288 pounds of pure gold, and a splendid ceremony of thanksgiving and dedication was held.

The Buddha's wooden temple was burned several times, and an earthquake shook the head off the statue, but it has been repaired and sits in massive dignity in its temple today. The Daibutsu is overwhelming because of its sheer bulk, but this smaller ancient Buddha in the Museum has a modest beauty that endears it to the beholder.

41

GEISHA DANCERS: FESTIVAL IN KYOTO

AT LAST we have a chance to see the fabled geishas of Japan. Here, dancing outdoors in the clear light of day, with nothing more ornamental than the plain tatami mats underfoot, these elegant creatures still have an aura of mystery, an atmosphere of luxury. It is the Emperor's birthday, and in Koyoto before the Heian (*hey*-YAHN) Shrine the geishas are dancing to celebrate the event. These women are highly trained artists —geisha means "cultured person"—who have served a long, hard apprenticeship in singing, dancing, flower arranging, literature, painting and music. Their dances are sedate and ceremonial, and they are robed in layers of kimonos.

Only very rich Japanese can afford to be entertained by geishas; a party at which a number of these artists entertains would be very costly. The geishas entertain their clients with songs, dances, and witty conversation.

The Japanese social system is very different from ours, and the geisha fills a need that we do not have in our society. The men of Japan do not habitually escort their wives in outside social activity with other men, yet they want feminine companionship when they are out together. The geisha has perfected witty and cultivated companionship into an art.

42

JAPANESE ARCHITECTURE: THE HEIAN SHRINE

LEAVING the geishas to their stately dance we wander around the famous garden at the rear of the shrine. This is Japanese architecture at its simple best, a graceful house in harmony with its natural site. The sweeping roof, borrowed from the Chinese, has been modified in Japan, and its tiny wooden shingles are a tribute to the carpenter's art. There are sliding doors made of wooden frames covered with paper, and the entire front of a Japanese house can be opened to "let the garden enter the house." Western architects have admired the beauty and livability of these buildings, and we are beginning to see the Japanese influence more and more in our own houses.

The Heian Shrine was built in 1895 to commemorate the founding of Kyoto over a thousand years before. The capital was moved from Nara twenty-six miles away to what was then known as Heian (Peace and Calmness). As the new capital grew its name was changed to Kyoto (Metropolis), and that fits the city today. Kyoto is the fourth-largest city in Japan with a population of 1,200,000. Because it was the capital of the court until Emperor Meiji moved to Tokyo in 1868, it has a very rich cultural and artistic background. This interesting city is additionally famous today for its silks, porcelains, lacquer ware and prints.

The "frozen music" of Chinese roofs was borrowed centuries ago by admiring Japanese.

45

SHOOTING
THE RAPIDS:
HOZU RIVER

EVEN if there were no tourists from outside of Japan, the country would be swept by tides of native travelers visiting the historic and scenic places of their own land. One of the most popular spots is the Hozu (*hoh-zoo*) River just outside of Kyoto. The Japanese enjoy combining a pilgrimage to the city's famous shrines and temples with a nature pilgrimage —the two are closely associated in their thinking.

The Hozu River cuts through deep gorges and narrow valleys, winding sharply and punctuated with foaming rapids. Flat-bottomed boats maneuvered by men with long oars take passengers on the thrilling descent of the river. Along the way, the rocky hillsides hang above the water, with an occasional small shrine perched among the pine trees. When the boat negotiates Lion's Mouth, or skirts the whirlpool with a rock at its center, the passengers are probably grateful for the comforting presence of these rural shrines.

In spring there are cherry trees in bloom, in early summer the hills are bright with wild azaleas, and in autumn the rich deep tones of the

In northern Japan one of the joys of winter is building a little snow house for a cozy tea party.

maple leaves color the valley. As long ago as the thirteenth century a Japanese monk wrote, "My only desire for this life is to see the beauties of the changing seasons." His compatriots still share that sentiment, and part of their delight in nature comes from an appreciation of its changing moods reflected in the seasons.

TERRACED FARMLAND: THE PRECIOUS EARTH

WAVING fields of wheat and stands of corn "as high as an elephant's eye" will never be seen in Japan. We have only to look at this picture to realize at once how different from ours is the Japanese agriculture. Where we have vast acres under mechanical cultivation, Japanese farms resemble gardens with each small plot bearing the meticulous stamp of hand labor. Because of the hilly and mountainous terrain only a small proportion of Japan's total land area is under cultivation. Farmers have carefully terraced some of the unlevel land, and not a scrap of ground goes to waste. Furthermore Japanese farms are coaxed into yielding two and sometimes three crops a year.

Since the war, land reforms have been instituted that make the farmer's lot a happier one. Electricity has come to the rural areas, and some houses even enjoy the boon of radio and television. The farmer and his wife can now come in from a backbreaking day in the fields where each plant has been cared for by hand according to the most ancient methods—then a flick of the switch and the paper-walled house resounds to the marvelous racket of the twentieth century.

There is one thing about Japanese farmlands that well might strike envy into the hearts of American farmers. Do you see how green the land is, with no bare or dusty patches? The Japanese people had a reverence for their trees and never deforested the hills. As a result, their land is seldom washed out by flood waters rolling down the naked hills. Though the farmer has precious little land, it might comfort him to know that he gets more, much more, from every acre than his European or American counterparts.

MASTER PUPPETEER: OSAKA'S FAMED THEATER

THE city of Osaka has a double fame. It is Japan's leading industrial metropolis, and it is also the dramatic center of a country long devoted to the theater. In this picture we see the gifted practitioners of one of the oldest and most unusual of Japan's dramatic arts. The puppet theater in Osaka goes back three hundred years or more, and is as far removed from our Punch and Judy shows as grand opera is from burlesque. In the seventeenth century the playwright Monzaemon (*mohn-zye-mohn*), who was the Shakespeare of Japan, wrote for the puppet theater. And there was a time when these remarkable dolls were even more popular than live actors. So great was their influence that the Kabuki (*kah-*BOO*-kee*) actors today move jerkily and assume the stiff attitudes of puppets—the final tribute of nature imitating art.

The Bunrakuza (*boon-rah-koo-zah*) Theater in Osaka is the home of the famous puppet drama. The puppets are two-thirds life-size, made of plaster and bamboo, and costumed in classical robes of gorgeous silk and brocade. The eyes, eyebrows, mouth—even the lips and tongue and every finger joint—are articulated realistically. It takes three men to manipulate such a complicated puppet. The master puppeteer is dressed in a splendid costume but his two assistants wear black hoods and robes. Body, head and right hand are controlled by the master. Only the feet and left hand are entrusted to the assistants. A narrator singsongs the dialogue and describes the action, while another man plunks at a samisen, a sort of square Japanese banjo.

The astonishing thing about Bunraku, the name for these puppet shows, is that there is no attempt made to conceal the three men who operate each puppet. Yet they invest the doll with such life and personality that the audience can be moved to tears by its activities. The theater magic is so potent that during the play, when a puppet makes its exit, it appears to be pulling the puppeteers off stage with it.

OSAKA AT NIGHT: PACHINKO DEN

IF THE Japanese countryside is lovely by daylight, her big cities acquire a special beauty at night. The noise, the crowds, the tawdry and tinseled atmosphere of many of the streets are transformed when darkness falls. Then the streets bloom with colored lights, and the frequent showers make dark mirrors of the pavements. What was an ugly imitation of a Western city in the daytime becomes mysterious and poetically Oriental after dark.

Here is Osaka, a businessman's city of two million people, on a rainy evening. It looks like an enchanted grotto. As a matter of fact, the place in this picture casts a particularly powerful spell of enchantment over many Japanese. It is a *pachinko* (*pah-cheen-koh*) den—the name is spelled with a "k" in spite of the neon lettering—and the craze for this pinball game has spread throughout the country. Players buy 500 metal balls at a clip and, releasing them one by one, they try to get them to drop into one of the lucky holes. The prizes are trivial—sweets, toys, soap or fruit. Looking into a *pachinko* den you see the players standing before rows of machines like automatons, squandering precious yen in the hopes of winning trash. And outside, above the shuffling sound of feet, the cries of vendors, the blare of music, you can hear the monotonous rattle and click of the little steel balls, an empty and unproductive sound in the night.

The Japanese Sandman and the lullaby of the pachinko balls are putting Junior to sleep. He may be bored, but his mama isn't.

ASHIBE DANCERS: GEISHA THEATRICAL PERFORMANCE

THE famous Takarazuka girls have their own theater not far from Osaka, but every spring the geishas take over a theater in that city and put on their own spectacular performances. Their dances are based on the sad old stories of Japan, but the costuming and staging are dazzlingly gay.

The Japanese have found it difficult to enjoy Western dramas in which ordinary people sit around in everyday clothes, sometimes in squalid rooms, and talk, talk, talk. Their No (*noh*) plays are slow-paced, symbolic and highly stylized. The actors wear masks and speak in muffled unnatural voices. Furthermore they speak an ancient courtly Japanese incomprehensible to most of the audience. Gesture, costume and music are what count.

The Kabuki theater is more popular than the severely classical No, but by Western standards it is still a slow-moving and strange performance. Nevertheless, the Kabuki actors have gone on tour, and have had successful engagements outside Japan. The remarkable costumes and fantastic make-up, worn by actors who can skillfully transmit emotion, are exciting even to audiences who do not understand the story.

The plot of the Ashibe performance that is pictured here is typical. The girl in white is a beautiful princess who lived thirteen hundred years ago. The program notes explain, "She ended her short life of 29 years which were full of sorrow, but never lost faith in the love of Buddha until the last day of her life." We follow the princess through twelve lavish scenes, arriving at last at this finale. After almost being murdered, nearly committing suicide, and becoming a nun, our princess has at last succeeded in weaving a picture of Buddha with lotus thread. We can see it in tableau behind her. The entire performance is one to bewitch and stir the senses.

54

OSAKA CASTLE: SHOGUN'S CITADEL

REFLECTED in the calm waters of its moat, the Osaka Castle looks peaceful enough today. But it was situated in a strategic military spot and its history is told in blood, fire and personal tragedy. The castle was built in the sixteenth century by the shogun Hideyoshi (*hee-*DEH-*yoh-shee*) as a military stronghold. He kept his generals busy in a competition to supply him with the massive stone blocks needed for its original construction. We can see some of the huge rocks in the lower section of the castle—all that survived when the superstructure was destroyed in 1868. This majestic building was reconstructed in 1931, and it retains the imposing strength of the original.

After Hideyoshi died, a war broke out between his son and his most able general, Iyeyasu Tokugawa, of whom we have heard before. Iyeyasu raised an enormous army of over a million and a quarter men and laid siege to Osaka Castle. The mighty stronghold fell when the despairing son and his mother committed suicide within its walls. The Tokugawas ran Japan from that time until the Restoration of 1868. Then their troops, retreating from the citadel, set fire to it and destroyed the ancient symbol of their power. Today the five-storied castle is equipped with elevators—an effete modern convenience that would have shocked the tough old warriors. The stronghold is now a museum guarding mementoes of bygone days of glory.

Feudal Japan comes to life again in the strange old music of the dragon flute.

PILGRIMS AT
SHODO ISLAND:
PORT ON THE
INLAND SEA

ONE of the loveliest trips in all Japan is the voyage from Osaka by ship through the Inland Sea. This narrow island-flecked stretch of water is sheltered by Honshu, Shikoku and Kyushu. It is a miniature Mediterranean, with warm beaches, small fishing villages and hundreds of piney green islands poking up out of deep blue water. When we travel through this part of Japan we realize what an important part the sea plays in the life of the country. Fleets of fishing boats, most of them motorized but many still under sail, create picturesque water traffic. Sea food forms a large part of the Japanese diet, and fishing is one of the major industries of the country.

In this picture we see one of the islands called Shodo (SHOH-*doh*), which lies off the larger island of Shikoku. In the background you can see the incredible blue of the water reflecting the clear clean skies. Shodo is a rocky island whose quarries have been famous over the centuries. Much of the stone with which Osaka Castle was built came from here. It is possible that the shogun felt happier with a good stretch of sea between him and his generals, and so he set them to chopping rocks for him on Shodo.

Many Japanese visit this scenic island in autumn when the maple leaves are at their brilliant best. Then there are special ferry boats to accommodate the crowds of nature-lovers who cluster here thick as autumn leaves themselves. At almost any season there will be a few pilgrims, like those we see here, climbing along the island's paths on a devout visit to its shrines. Shinto, the native religion of Japan, combines a worship of nature with ancestor worship, and among its eight million gods there are deities of the sea, rivers, mountains, wind and trees. In a way these pilgrims, rejoicing in the beauty of the day and of their surroundings, are at worship long before they reach their shrine.

PATIENT WATER BUFFALO: WORKING THE RICE PADDIES

RICE is the staff of life for the Japanese, and in the old days income was even figured and paid in units of this indispensable food. Of its twelve million acres of land under cultivation Japan uses seven million for rice. As we can see in this picture, rice paddies have to be flooded during most of the season, and the muddy surface soil must be stirred up before the rice seedlings can be transplanted. Since it is not possible to mechanize the process, a water buffalo, the favorite farm animal of Asia, is used to plod through the mud, pulling a primitive plow.

On the smaller hilly islands sweet potatoes are easier to grow than rice, and they form a large part of the diet of the poorer classes. To offer a meal including sweet potatoes to a guest is an insult in Japan, where rice has become a status symbol. The Japanese have a discriminating appreciation for their basic food, and they esteem rice grown at home more highly than the "foreign rice" that must be imported from abroad. The Emperor himself offers special prayers for the success of the rice crop when the farmers begin their sowing in February. The first offering of the new crop is made to the gods in October, and in November there is an important ceremony of the tasting of the new rice by the Emperor and the people. To the Japanese this simple fare is considered food for the gods and their ruler.

Children are treasured in Japan, and the first years of their lives are spent regarding the world from mother's safe strong back.

61

LONG-TAILED ROOSTER: ORNAMENTAL BIRD OF KOCHI

O N THE island of Shikoku, in the little town of Kochi (кон-*chee*), we find one of the interesting curiosities of Japan. This is where they breed the *onagadori* (*oh-nah-gah-doh-ree*), or long-tailed roosters. These strange birds serve no useful function today, although in feudal times the lords and warriors used them. In their processions of state, the samurai marched carrying long lances, and fluttering from the tops of them were the twenty-foot ribbons of plumes from the tails of these fabulous birds.

The breeders of the *onagadori* put a price on their birds based upon the length of the tail feathers. They charge about $2.00 a foot, and the longest plumes on record measured 24 feet. There is undoubtedly a very limited market for forty-dollar roosters, especially since their care poses problems. The bird is kept in a tall narrow cage, and its precious tail is either coiled and wrapped in cloth or looped over a hanger. Every three days the rooster is exercised. Then it is taken out for a walk, and an attendant must follow behind it carrying the tail like a royal train-bearer. There is evidently a special appeal about a creature bred for rarity and beauty, whose only function is to excite wonder and admiration in the beholder. It is interesting that these birds still exist in a country that has become industrialized and westernized so rapidly. It must mean that the old values still prevail at the heart and core of Japan.

The stout white hemp rope worn by the stout sumo wrestler is a badge of his championship and moral integrity.

62

SUMO DOG:
CANINE
WRESTLING CHAMP

ANOTHER oddity that we find in Kochi is the *sumo* (soo-MOH) dog. These powerful beasts are a breed called Tosa dogs, and they are trained as fighters of a very special sort. Anyone who has ever witnessed a dogfight knows it as a growling, snarling, slashing battle between two furies. But the *sumo* dogs are trained to fight as much like *sumo* wrestlers as is possible for a four-footed animal. They try for wrestling holds, and the first dog who whimpers, growls or barks, loses the fight. If there is no decision after five minutes, the fight is stopped.

In this picture one of the champions is posing in full *sumo* regalia with his handlers, who are more modestly attired. *Sumo* (for human contestants) is an ancient sport in Japan, said to be over 1500 years old. It is performed by obese giants who weigh from 250 to 450 pounds, and seem to bear little physical resemblance to the average Japanese, who is slight and slender. Usually a boy huskier or taller than the average decides to become a *sumo* wrestler. A special diet—these wrestlers eat ten times the quantity most Japanese eat, and drink beer and sake in prodigious amounts—and rigorous exercise develop the boys into heavily fleshed, powerfully muscled men. They wear their long hair in a samurai topknot, and their wrestling garb is a dark loincloth. The more elaborate the cloth, the higher the wrestler's rank.

A *sumo* tournament begins early in the morning and lasts until evening. The nearly naked giants go through a ritual of limbering exercises and stylized prayers. They scatter salt in the ring to purify it, and then begin a long period of preparatory approaches. An actual bout may take only a minute or so, as a contestant wins as soon as his opponent touches the ground with any part of his body but his feet. *Sumo*, as you might guess, has had a great resurgence of popularity lately. This ancient sport is a natural for modern television.

TRANSPLANTING RICE SEEDLINGS: WOMEN FARMERS

JAPANESE women, for all their apparent delicacy, do much of the country's heavy and difficult work. This picture shows a not uncommon view of the Orient—the trousered feminine figure under a broad-brimmed straw hat, stooping patiently over a flooded rice paddy, her image reflected in its pewter surface. A month or more after the rice seeds have been sown in a bed, the seedlings must be painstakingly pulled and transplanted by hand in flooded fields. Sometimes they are planted in deep marshes, and then the women stand chest deep in icy muddy water for five and six hours at a stretch. They are better suited to this work than men because it is believed that their bodies are better able to stand the cold.

For that reason Japanese women are used as divers for seaweed, abalone and pearls. They dive for an hour, then revive themselves before a fire for two hours. In the cultured-pearl industry the diving girls must find and bring to the surface the young oysters which will play host to an irritant that becomes a pearl. These girls, dressed in white to frighten off sharks, can stay under water for as long as two minutes at a time. At Pearl Island you can watch them demonstrate their difficult skill, developed so that other women in other parts of the world can own pearls at a relatively low cost.

Less glamorous than their deep-sea sisters are the women in fishing villages who launch the heavy boats and later pull them up on the beach. A crew of a hundred or more women also hauls in the heavy nets that have been spread in the water by the male crews. Japanese girls know that their traditional position is one of waiting on the men of the family, and in the farming and fishing communities their duties are extended to include much of the arduous work outside the home.

GATEWAY TO MIYAJIMA: SHRINE ISLAND

THIS is one of the most memorable sights of the Inland Sea voyage. Against a background of hazy blue mountains, rising magically from the calm water is the vermilion torii that is the gateway to Miyajima (MEE-*ah-jee*-MAH), or Shrine Island. The island itself is venerated by the Japanese, most of whom hope to visit its Shinto shrine at least once in their lifetime. At high tide the boats coming to Miyajima sail under the huge torii, a fitting entrance to the shrine of a maritime people. This camphor-wood gateway was built in 1875, but the main shrine on the island has been in existence for at least a thousand years, although the buildings have been reconstructed from time to time.

The torii stands about 500 feet from the shore, and the shrine buildings are set in a little cove. The buildings are connected by broad wooden walks built on piles, and when the tide is in, the shrine seems to float on the surface of the sea. The vermilion buildings take on an added brilliance against the deep green of the island's virgin forest. For the trees of Miyajima are no less sacred than the holy shrine, and no ax has ever touched them.

The priest at Miyajima may frighten away devils with his fearsome dance, but he attracts tourists, both native and foreign.

The Shinto priests perform ceremonial dances here that are quite remarkable. Dressed in elaborate robes whose color and ornateness match the shrine, the priests are masked in grotesque headpieces. They enact an ancient and terrifying pantomime designed to frighten devils from the shrine.

HIROSHIMA: ATOM BOMB MONUMENT

FOURTEEN miles from Shrine Island at the head of a wide bay is the city of Hiroshima (HEE-*roh-shee*-MAH). Originally its name meant "broad island," but in the twentieth century Hiroshima has gained another connotation. On August 6, 1945, when an atomic bomb was dropped on this city, Hiroshima became a symbol of the terrible power of destruction which so concerns the world today. In the years since the bomb fell, Hiroshima has rebuilt itself into a thriving city, but it is now a city with a message—Peace.

In 1947 the citizens held their first Peace Festival, and it has become an important yearly event. A Peace Avenue and Peace Hall are planned, and the Hiroshima Peace City Construction Committee has organized the rebuilding of the city with substantial help from the Japanese government. The new Hiroshima has dedicated itself to setting an example to the rest of the world.

We are looking at the one ruined building that will remain in the new city. This was the Industry Promotion Hall, and its twisted walls mark the pinpoint spot of the target over which the bomb exploded. At first the section of the city that came within a two-mile radius of this gaunt skeleton was called the Atomic Desert, and no one thought life could return to it for a long time. But within two years the land began to revive. Among the blasted trees new shoots put out green leaves, and we can see the hopeful portents of new life in this picture.

Today 400,000 people live in Hiroshima—the same number as before the war. And it is once again the most important industrial, educational and communications center of western Japan.

CARP STREAMERS: BOYS' FESTIVAL DECORATIONS

BOLDLY outlined against the Hiroshima sky, the carp flags are happy symbols of a Japanese holiday. It is May 5th, Boys' Day, and throughout the length and breadth of Japan, families with sons are celebrating.

Little girls have their holiday, too, the Doll Festival in March. But today is for the boys. It is also called the Iris Festival because the leaf of that flower is shaped like a sword blade, and every boy carries a wooden "iris sword" on this day. The festival is centuries old, and it is designed to remind boys of the manly virtues of bravery and strength. If a family has any military heirlooms belonging to a brave ancestor, this is the day they are brought out. Swords, helmets or armor are on display in the *tokonoma* (*toh-koh-noh-mah*), the alcove devoted to a flower arrangement and the one or two most beautiful objects in the home.

But outside the house, for the whole world to see, each family erects a long bamboo pole. One carp is flown for each son, and the eldest boy—always the most important child in a Japanese family—has the largest one. These colorful paper fish swimming bravely against the wind are symbolic of real carp who fight their way upstream with determination. They are a perfect example to young boys who must have the ambition and strength to fight their way up through the difficulties of childhood to manhood.

Strips of newly dyed silk flap gaily in the sunshine . . . proud banners of one of Japan's great industries.

73

TORTOISE-SHELL ARTIST: NAGASAKI SPECIALTY

JAPANESE sons grow up to learn the crafts of their fathers, and the secrets of the old masters are jealously kept within the family. The artist we see here has a lifetime of skill in those old and clever hands, but more than that he has the traditions of generations of men in his own family that have been transmitted to him. The exquisite objects of tortoise-shell ware for which Nagasaki is famous have been created by the same families for hundreds of years.

Almost anything the Japanese put their hands to they make with consummate skill. They have been borrowers rather than innovators, learning their arts and crafts from Korean and Chinese teachers centuries ago, and acquiring their knowledge of modern industrial products from the West in this past century. Just as the Japanese became adept at making beautiful silks and these tortoise-shell delicacies, so they have become wizards at turning out lenses and precision instruments today. Their traditional reverence for fine craftsmanship is the underlying reason for their astonishing success. And it stems from the ancient family structure and religion in Japan.

Every family had its special occupation—farmer, actor, flower-arranger, calligrapher, doctor, soldier or humble artisan. And just as there were family gods, there were also gods presiding over every occupation from the highest to the lowest. So when an artist made a ship of tortoise shell, his workmanship had to be fine enough to honor the father who taught him and the god who ruled over his very tools. The needle of a seamstress was no less sacred than the sword of a samurai warrior.

Watching this artist create a beautiful object we are aware of an atmosphere of harmony. The place where he works is as attractive as the products made there. The tools he uses are as finely crafted and designed as the boxes and combs they have formed. And the man himself has the rapt and peaceful look of someone at his devotions.

74

SHIPYARDS AT NAGASAKI: BOOMING INDUSTRY

NAGASAKI, lying on the west coast of the island of Kyushu, is one of the loveliest maritime sites in the world. Steep wooded hills shelter it on three sides, and on the fourth it is open to the long blue expanse of Nagasaki Bay. Up this bay in the sixteenth century sailed the first ships to bring Japan into contact with the West. Spanish, Portuguese and Dutch traders introduced the science and culture and Christianity of Europe to Japan through Nagasaki, the only port open to them. Eventually it, too, was closed to all but a few Dutch and Chinese, when Japan retreated into her long feudal isolation.

The romance of this city where East and West meet inspired Puccini's opera, "Madame Butterfly." And the impact of European science and technology is reflected in the modern shipyards stretching for miles along the scenic bay. In 1945 Japan's industrial plants were almost hopelessly crippled and her merchant fleet had been wiped from the seas. Now the Japanese are saying, "The postwar period is over!" Heavy industry has not only recovered, it has progressed. And Japan's merchant fleet ranks fourth in the world for number of ships. The busy shipyards are producing vessels that will sail under many flags, making Japan the largest shipbuilding country in the world. The speed and extent of the country's recovery have been due in no small measure to the perfectionism and skill of her craftsmen. Generations have been bred to use their hands well, and it is the hands of present-day Japanese that are rebuilding their country.

The tapering Japanese hand has been shaped by centuries of disciplined use, until now it is capable of infinitely precise workmanship.

SAYONARA TO JAPAN: A BEAUTY TO REMEMBER

IN spite of its growing industrial might, Japan remains in the minds of most of us an essentially feminine country. The grace and courtesy that are native to all Japanese are most apparent to us in Japanese women. And Japan's greatest charm for the visitor is personified by a dainty girl wrapped in a kimono. Although most Japanese men wear Western-style clothes, many women still dress in kimonos, and without them the country would lose much of its distinctive color. The fact that the garment has to be completely taken apart and resewn every time it is washed does not deter them. A beautiful and graceful tradition is worth the effort.

And there, perhaps, is the secret of the best values that have endured in Japanese life in spite of many drastic changes. Factories and motorcycles and bars and blue jeans have had their undeniable effect upon a gracious civilization. But the fine old ways are still treasured, and the delicacy and flowerlike charm of Japanese women are still cherished. Lafcadio Hearn, writing about Japan at the turn of the century,

The more Japan changes, the more it is the same. Old beauties—as well as young ones—will continue to be important factors in the country's life.

said, "The most wonderful aesthetic products of Japan are not its ivories, nor its bronzes, nor its porcelains, nor its swords, nor any of its marvels in metal or lacquer—but its women." As we say "Sayonara" (good-by) to the young lady we see here, we can only agree.

SOME IMPORTANT DATES IN JAPANESE HISTORY

c. 3,000 B.C.	*Primitive tribes—believed to be possible predecessors of the aboriginal Ainus — come to Japan via Siberia and the Kuril Islands. Later invasions from Southern Asia bring a more advanced people who eventually take over the islands.*
400 A.D.	*Beginning of written history. Japanese officially adopt Chinese script.*
552	*Korean king introduces Buddhism to Japanese Court.*
710-793	*The Nara Period is established by the Empress Gemmyo. Arts and literature flourish in Nara, first permanent capital.*
794-1185	*Heian Period. Capital moves from Nara to Kyoto. The Fujiwara family, acting as regents, dominate the Emperors of Japan.*
1185-1336	*The Kamakura Period. Bushido, the Way of the Warrior, becomes an important part of Japanese life, and Kamakura is the military capital.*
1192	*Yoritomo Minamoto establishes complete military power. Becomes the first shogun. The shogunate lasts until mid-nineteenth century.*
1545	*Portuguese traders come to Japan from Macao, first Europeans to establish relations.*
1549	*Francis Xavier arrives in Japan to teach the tenets of the Jesuits. Some Japanese are converted to Christianity.*
1605	*Dutch are granted permission to trade in Japan; English receive similar grant in 1613.*
1616-1853	*Tokugawa shoguns close Japan to foreigners.*
1853	*Commodore Matthew C. Perry of the United States Navy lands in Japan. On his return in 1854, .U.S. signs first trade treaty with Japan at Yokohama. Policy of seclusion ends.*
1868-1912	*The Meiji Restoration. Under Emperor Meiji, Tokyo becomes the capital; the shogunate system ends, and with it the feudal system.*
1894-1895	*The Sino-Japanese War.*
1904-1905	*The Russo-Japanese War.*
1914-1917	*World War I. Japan enters war with Allies, and later is instrumental in the formation of the League of Nations.*
1937	*"The China Incident." Japan launches attack on China.*
Sept. 27, 1940	*Japan signs tripartite pact with Italy and Germany, formally becomes an Axis power.*
Dec. 7, 1941	*The Japanese attack Pearl Harbor. United States and allies declare war on the Japanese Empire.*
Sept. 2, 1945	*The Japanese formally surrender aboard the battleship Missouri. Second World War ends.*
1945-1951	*Occupation by Allied forces under General MacArthur.*
May 3, 1947	*The new constitution establishes a democratic government in Japan with the Emperor as a figurehead.*
Sept. 8, 1951	*United States and 48 other nations sign a peace treaty with Japan.*

SOME FAMOUS NAMES IN JAPANESE HISTORY

EMPEROR JIMMU (711-585 B.C.)—*Established Japan's imperial line. Ascended the throne in 660 B.C., according to Japanese mythology.*

PRINCE SHOTOKU TAISHI (573-621 A.D.)—*One of Japan's greatest leaders; responsible for the introduction of Chinese culture to Japan. Later initiated diplomatic relations between China and Japan (607).*

KAMATARI FUJIWARA (614-669)—*The first member of the powerful family of court statesmen. Opposed Buddhism and fought to keep the Japanese belief in Shintoism. The Fujiwara maintained their position as advisors to the Emperor for several centuries.*

MURASAKI SHIKIBU (c.978-c.1031)—*Japanese authoress. This lady-in-waiting to Empress Ichijo wrote the* Tale of Genji, *one of the world's great works of literature.*

YORITOMO MINAMOTO (1147-1199)—*Established the first shogunate, or military court, in Japan. The shogunate marked the passing of the supreme executive power from the hands of the Emperor to the rising class of military leaders.*

KAN-NAMI KIYOTSUGU (1333-1384)—*Innovator of Japan's No drama; his son Se-Ami Motokiyo, actor and playwright, was largely instrumental in bringing the ancient No drama to its present form.*

ODA NOBUNAGA (1534-1582)—*Member of the Taira military clan. Began the unification of Japan by crushing the power of the Japanese war lords.*

HIDEYOSHI TOYOTOMI (1536-1598)—*Japan's leading military strategist of medieval times. Continued the process of unification begun by Nobunaga. His regime marked period of great artistic achievement, including the beginning of Kabuki theater.*

IYEYASU TOKUGAWA (1542-1616)—*Took over the shogunate upon Hideyoshi's death in 1598. The first political administrator to bring the whole of Japan under central control.*

MATSUO BASHO (1644-1694)—*One of the masters of Japanese hokku poetry, which flowered during the Edo period.*

EMPEROR MEIJI (Mutsuhito) (1852-1912)—*Leader of the Restoration, which launched the country on the course of Westernization and brought the Japanese out of a long period of isolation. Centralized the government; opened the ports to foreign commerce; made Tokyo the capital of the nation.*

EMPEROR HIROHITO (1901-   )—*The present reigning monarch of the Japanese empire. During his reign Japan's imperialist expansion to the mainland of Asia and the islands of the Pacific reached its pinnacle and collapsed. After World War II, his powers were transferred to the Japanese Diet, or Parliament.*

HIDEKI YUKAWA (1907-   )—*Japanese physicist. Discovered existence of electrons hitherto unknown in atomic nucleus. Awarded Nobel Prize in 1949.*

SOME JAPANESE WORDS AND PHRASES

Here is a list of words and phrases that you might be likely to use when traveling in Japan. The anglicized spelling of the Japanese words is based on the Hepburn system. The words are then written in simple phonetics with the accented syllable in small capitals.

I do not understand	Wakari masen (*wah-*KAH-*ree mah-*SEN)
Please speak slowly	Yukkuri hanashite kudasai (*yoo-*KOO-*ree hah-*NAH-*sh'teh koo-dah-*SAH-*ee*)
Please help me	Tasukete kudasai (*tah-*SKET-*eh koo-dah-*SAH-*ee*)
Help!	Tasukete! (*tah-*SKET-*eh*)
I am lost	Michini mayotta (*mee-chee-*NEE *mah-*YOHT-*tah*)
Please show me	Oshiete kudasai (*oh-shee-eh-*TEH *koo-dah-*SAH-*ee*)
Thank you	Arigato (*ah-*REE-*gah-toh*)
You're welcome	Doitashimashite (DOH-*ee-tah-shee-mah-shee-teh*)
Please	Dozo (DOH-*zoh*)
Excuse me	Shitsurei (SH'TSOO-*reh-ee*)
How are you?	Ikaga desu ka? (*ee-*KAH-*gah* DEHS *kah*)
I am well	Genki desu (GHEN-*kee dehs*)
I am hungry	Onaka-ga sukimashita (*oh-nah-kah-*GAH *soo-kee-*MAH-*shee-tah*)
I am thirsty	Nodo-ga kawakimashita (*noh-doh-*GAH *kah-wah-kee-*MAH-*shee-tah*)
Where is a hotel?	Yadoya wa doko desu ka? (Japanese style) (*yah-doh-*YAH *wah doh-koh* DEHS *kah*)
	Hoteru wa doko desu ka? (European style) (*hoh-teh-roo wah doh-koh* DEHS *kah*)
Where is a restaurant?	Shokudo wa doko desu ka? (*shoh-koo-*DOH *wah doh-koh* DEHS *kah*)
How can I get there?	Dosureba sokoe yukare masu ka? (DOH-*soo-reh-bah soh-koh-*EH *yoo-kah-*REH MAHS *kah*)
I want to buy............	.... o kaitai no desu (*oh kah-ee-*TAH-*ee noh dehs*)
I would like	.... ga hoshii no desu (*gah hoh-*SHEE-*ee noh dehs*)

FOOD AND DRINK

Food	tabemono (*tah-beh-moh-*NOH)
Water (drinking)	nomimizu (*noh-*MEE-*mee-zoo*)
Tea	ocha (*oh-*CHAH)
Coffee	kohi (*koh-*HEE)
Soup	suimono (*soo-ee-moh-*NOH)
Rice (cooked)	gohan (GOH-*hahn*)
Meat	niku (*nee-*KOO)
Pork	butaniku (*boo-*TAH-*nee-koo*)
Chicken	toriniku (*toh-*REE-*nee-koo*)
Eggs	tamago (*tah-*MAH-*goh*)
Fish	sakana (*sah-kah-*NAH)

MONEY

Yen	
Sen	100 sen to the yen

This elegant Japanese symbol means: *mind, idea, will.*

INDEX